STEP FORWARD WITH GRATITUDE

SHANNON WELBOURN

Crabtree Publishing Company
www.crabtreebooks.com

Author
Shannon Welbourn

Series research and development
Reagan Miller

Editorial director
Kathy Middleton

Editors
Reagan Miller, Janine Deschenes

Series Consultant
Larry Miller: BA (Sociology), BPE, MSc.Ed
Retired teacher, guidance counselor, and certified coach

Print and production coordinator
Katherine Berti

Design and photo research
Katherine Berti

Photographs
Shutterstock: © Tinseltown, p 8 (inset);
© Featureflash Photo Agency, p 9; © Free Wind 2014, p 12
Wikimedia: p 8 (inset bkgd)
Other images by Shutterstock

Library and Archives Canada Cataloguing in Publication

Welbourn, Shannon, author
    Step forward with gratitude / Shannon Welbourn.

(Step forward!)
Includes index.
Issued in print and electronic formats.
ISBN 978-0-7787-2784-2 (hardback).--
ISBN 978-0-7787-2826-9 (paperback).--ISBN 978-1-4271-1830-1 (html)

    1. Gratitude--Juvenile literature. I. Title.

BF575.G68W45 2016   j158.1   C2016-903359-7
                                            C2016-903360-0

Library of Congress Cataloging-in-Publication Data

Names: Welbourn, Shannon, author.
Title: Step forward with gratitude / Shannon Welbourn.
Description: New York : Crabtree Publishing Company, [2017] |
    Series: Step forward! | Includes index.
Identifiers: LCCN 2016034717 (print) | LCCN 2016043367 (ebook) |
    ISBN 9780778727842 (reinforced library binding : alk. paper) |
    ISBN 9780778728269 (pbk. : alk. paper) |
    ISBN 9781427118301 (Electronic HTML)
Subjects: LCSH: Gratitude in children--Juvenile literature. |
    Gratitude--Juvenile literature.
Classification: LCC BF723.G7 W45 2017 (print) | LCC BF723.G7 (ebook) |
    DDC 179/.9--dc23
LC record available at https://lccn.loc.gov/2016034717

Crabtree Publishing Company
www.crabtreebooks.com   1-800-387-7650

Printed in Canada/102016/IH20160811

Copyright © **2017 CRABTREE PUBLISHING COMPANY.** All rights reserved. No part of this publication may be reproduced, stored in a retrieval system or be transmitted in any form or by any means, electronic, mechanical, photocopying, recording, or otherwise, without the prior written permission of Crabtree Publishing Company. In Canada: We acknowledge the financial support of the Government of Canada through the Canada Book Fund for our publishing activities.

Published in Canada
Crabtree Publishing
616 Welland Ave.
St. Catharines, Ontario
L2M 5V6

Published in the United States
Crabtree Publishing
PMB 59051
350 Fifth Avenue, 59th Floor
New York, New York 10118

Published in the United Kingdom
Crabtree Publishing
Maritime House
Basin Road North, Hove
BN41 1WR

Published in Australia
Crabtree Publishing
3 Charles Street
Coburg North
VIC 3058

CONTENTS

What is Gratitude?............4

Why is Gratitude Important?.......6

Biography: Taylor Swift...........8

Gratitude at Home 10

Gratitude at School.............12

Gratitude in Your Community......14

Biography: Pay It Forward Day.....16

Overcoming Challenges..........18

Encouraging Gratitude In Others...20

Grow Your Gratitude!..........22

Learning More................23

Words to Know................24

Index........................24

About the Author...............24

WHAT IS GRATITUDE?

Do you know which two words are so powerful they can make you feel happier just by saying them? These two words are thank you!

We say thank you when someone does something kind or helpful. Saying thank you is one way to show gratitude. Gratitude is being aware of and thankful for the people, experiences, and things in our lives. These words show that we feel **grateful** for what they have done. Feeling grateful is also feeling happy about something good that has happened.

We can show gratitude by saying thank you or by doing something nice for someone.

Gratitude is an attitude, or way of thinking, that everyone can learn. Like learning anything new, it takes time and practice. Gratitude changes the way you see the world. It can help you at home, in school, and other areas of your life.

People who show gratitude are thankful for the everyday things and experiences in their lives.

WHY IS GRATITUDE IMPORTANT?

Gratitude makes people feel happy because they are aware of and appreciate **the people and things around them.**

You can build gratitude by learning to be **mindful**. Being mindful means paying close attention to what is happening right now. Often, people think about things that happened in the past, or things that will happen in the future. Being mindful helps you discover wonderful new things to be grateful for in the present moment. When you are with friends, try paying close attention to the funny stories they tell and how much they make you laugh. You will feel even more grateful that you are friends!

Being mindful helps your gratitude grow!

Think of a time that someone showed you gratitude. How did it make you feel? Gratitude helps us feel closer and more connected to our families and friends. Being mindul and appreciating the things around you also helps connect you to your **community** and the people in it.

Gratitude helps us appreciate the good things in our lives. It encourages us to give back to others.

Biography

TAYLOR SWIFT

Name: Taylor Swift

From: Wyomissing, Pennsylvania

Accomplishment: Shows her gratitude to her fans every day

Showing gratitude is important for everyone—even people who seem to have all that they could ever want!

Taylor Swift is a famous musician. She is very talented—but her success also comes from how well she treats her millions of fans around the world. Taylor's fans support her by listening to her music, buying tickets to her concerts, and following her on **social media**. Taylor feels grateful to her fans because they made her success possible. She shows her gratitude in many different ways, including mailing letters and gifts to fans and showing up at their birthday parties and events. She makes time to meet her fans to take pictures and chat with them.

Taylor has over 140 million followers on social media. She follows many of them back and often gives them words of encouragement!

"So to you, or anyone else who has spent four minutes on me in some way—listening to just one song, or watching one of my videos...Thank you."

—Taylor Swift

GRATITUDE AT HOME

What are you grateful to have in your home life?

Parents or other adults that care for us work hard to provide food, shelter, and other **basic needs**. We might not think about these things as often as we should. Saying thank you will make the people who work hard to care for you feel that you appreciate all that they do. When we thank someone, it's not enough to just say those two words. It's important to tell them what we are grateful for, such as telling your sister you are grateful that she helps you with your homework. Try practicing gratitude with your family by sitting together and telling each other reasons you are thankful.

Go around the table and say one thing you are grateful for that happened during the day, and then one reason you are grateful for a family member. This can help you and your family to be mindful of all the reasons you have to be grateful at home.

STEP FURTHER

Think of a reason you are grateful for each member of your family. Share your gratitude with them!

GRATITUDE AT SCHOOL

There are many reasons to show gratitude at school. Being able to go to school is something to be grateful for.

Some children around the world cannot go to school because they have to work to help support their families. Other children may have to travel far from their home to attend school.

*These students in Somalia don't always have enough **resources**, such as books and computers, to use at school—but they are grateful to go to school.*

Think about all of the resources you use at school. You write with pens and pencils, study from books, and work on computers. You have a desk and a classroom to learn in. These are all things to be grateful for. Maybe you are grateful for a teacher you really like, or a subject you always look forward to. Does a bus driver get you safely to and from school, or a school nurse help you feel better when you are sick? Making the decision to be thankful for the things you have at school helps you build gratitude.

GRATITUDE IN YOUR COMMUNITY

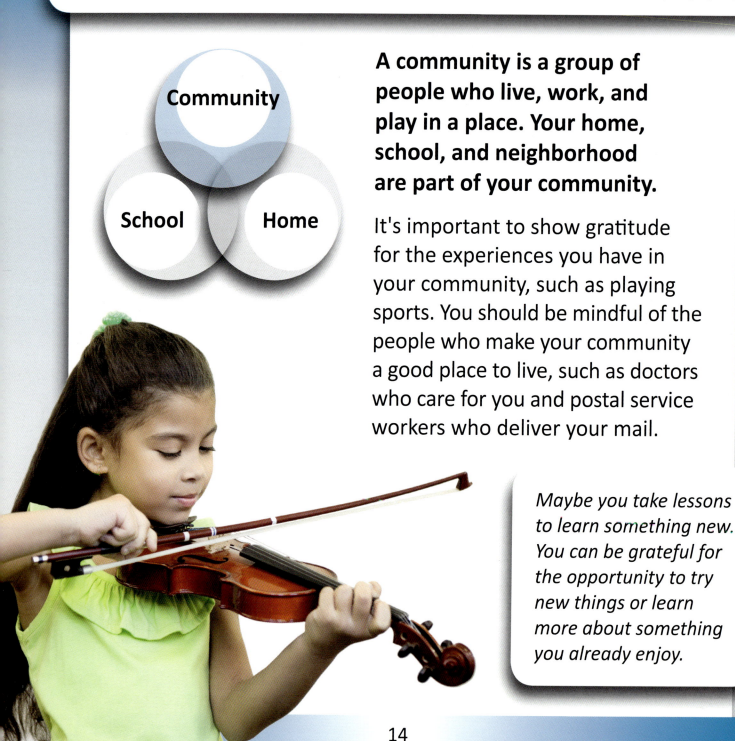

A community is a group of people who live, work, and play in a place. Your home, school, and neighborhood are part of your community.

It's important to show gratitude for the experiences you have in your community, such as playing sports. You should be mindful of the people who make your community a good place to live, such as doctors who care for you and postal service workers who deliver your mail.

Maybe you take lessons to learn something new. You can be grateful for the opportunity to try new things or learn more about something you already enjoy.

You can also show gratitude for the places in your community. Be mindful of the natural world around you, such as plants and animals that live in your community. You can show your gratitude for your community by **respecting** the natural world. You can also develop gratitude by visiting quiet places in your community to **reflect** on things you are thankful for. A calm, quiet space such as a park can be the perfect place to develop mindfulness and realize your appreciation for the places in your community.

Show your gratitude for your community by respecting the places, people, and other living things within it.

Biography

PAY IT FORWARD DAY

Name: Pay It Forward Day

From: Began in Australia, spread worldwide

Accomplishment: Encourages millions of people to show gratitude

Often, people who are grateful for the good in their lives also do things to help others. They do not expect anything in return. They are inspired to help and it makes them feel good to help others.

Pay It Forward Day is celebrated every year on the last Thursday of April. It gives everyone a chance to show their gratitude by helping others. Anyone can take part. All you need is an attitude for gratitude! On Pay It Forward Day, people show their gratitude by doing a good deed for someone and expecting nothing in return. The person who was helped by the good deed is encouraged to "pay it forward" through another good deed. This spreads gratitude far and wide!

The good deeds can be big or small. To show your gratitude, you can choose any good deed to do for any person you wish. Every helpful act counts! You don't need to wait for the next Pay it Forward Day. Here are some good deeds you might try.

One good deed leads to another and another as people pay it forward.

Help your brother with his paper route.

Bring a friend study notes when they are sick and miss class.

Water the garden for your grandpa.

Prepare lunch for your teacher or parent.

STEP FURTHER

On your own or with others, come up with three more ideas for ways to pay it forward!

OVERCOMING CHALLENGES

When we face problems or challenges, it can be difficult to remember to show gratitude for the things we have.

Being grateful can be challenging when we feel discouraged, angry, or worried. For example, if you are arguing with your brother or sister about what to watch on television, it can be easy to forget how grateful you felt when he or she helped you clean your room earlier in the day. Remembering reasons why you are grateful for people can help you overcome arguments.

Gratitude encourages forgiveness! Next time you have an argument, think of a reason why you are grateful for that person.

STEP FURTHER

Think back to a challenge you faced. Think of a reason you can be grateful for it.

When we experience challenges, we sometimes feel discouraged. Maybe your piano teacher was disappointed with you when you forgot to practice a new song for your lesson. The lesson was more difficult because you were not prepared. Sometimes we may not feel grateful for an experience at the time it happens, but we can look back later and see how it has helped us. That difficult piano lesson may have made you realize how helpful it is to be prepared. Now you always make sure to take time to practice.

ENCOURAGING GRATITUDE IN OTHERS

Being aware of your own gratitude helps you be happier. You can be a reason why someone else feels grateful, too!

Think of a way that you have thanked someone. When you show your gratitude to others, you encourage them to also **express** when they are thankful. Help others think of reasons why they are grateful for the people, experiences, and things in their lives. Encourage them to be mindful and appreciate everything they already have. Explain the reasons why you are grateful for others. Tell them how they make you feel. Then, "pay it forward" by doing something nice for them, and be a reason why they are grateful!

STEP FURTHER

Together with friends, come up with a list of reasons why you are thankful for each other.

GROW YOUR GRATITUDE!

One way to grow your gratitude is to show your gratitude!

It is important to take the time to show your gratitude to the people who deserve it. You may think that people already know how much you appreciate them. What if they don't? By taking the time to show your gratitude, you can be sure people know how you feel.

"Feeling gratitude and not expressing it is like wrapping a present and not giving it."

—William Arthur Ward, Writer

Name the Person

Think of all the people who care about you and help you reach your goals. These people may include family members, teachers, friends, tutors, and coaches.

You Choose

You can show your gratitude in different ways. For example, you can tell the person, write a letter, make a card, sing a song, write a poem, the choice is yours!

Be Specific

No matter how you choose to show your gratitude, you must be specific. Saying "thank you" is a good start, but it is important to describe the reasons why you are grateful. Think about:
- What did the person do?
- How did they help you or make a difference?

LEARNING MORE

BOOKS

Clayton, Dallas. *An Awesome Book of Thanks!* Two Lions, 2010.

DiOrio, Rana & Wheeler, Eliza. *What Does It Mean To Be Present?* Little Pickle Press, 2010.

Mora, Pat. *Gracias/Thanks.* Lee & Low Books, 2009.

Silverstein, Shel. *The Giving Tree.* Harper Collins, 2014

WEBSITES

www.growingwithgratitude.com
This website introduces the Growing with Gratitude program which helps teachers, students, and families develop the habits of gratitude.

www.relaxinside.com
Use this site to practice mindfulness by yourself, with family and friends, or in your classroom.

http://inspiremykids.com/2016/gratefulness-find-some-today
This link from the Inspire My Kids site includes a gratitude-inspiring video.

WORDS TO KNOW

appreciate [uh-PREE-shee-eyt] verb To feel or show thanks
basic needs [BEY-sic needs] noun The things, such as food, shelter, and water, that a person needs to survive, or stay alive
community [kuh-MYOO-ni-tee] noun A group of people who live, work, and play in a place
express [ik-SPRES] verb To state something aloud, in words
grateful [GREYT-fuh l] adjective Thankful or appreciative
mindful [MAHYND-fuhl] adjective Describing someone who is attentive, aware, or careful of what is going on around them
reflect [ri-FLEKT] verb To think back on something
resources [REE-sawrs-es] noun Supplies or support needed to do something
respect [ri-SPEKT] verb The act of giving something or someone the attention it deserves
social media [SOH-shuh l MEE-dee-uh] noun Websites or applications where people share information and communicate with each other

INDEX

basic needs 7, 10
community 7, 14, 15
home 10, 11, 14
mindfulness 6, 11, 12, 13, 14, 15, 20
Pay It Forward Day 16, 17
reflect 15, 19
relationships 7
school 12, 13, 14
Swift, Taylor 8, 9

ABOUT THE AUTHOR

Shannon Welbourn is a freelance author of educational K-12 books. She holds an honors BA in Child & Youth Studies, and is a certified teacher. Shannon works full-time as a Library and Media Specialist. In this position, she works closely with teachers and teacher candidates, helping to inspire and develop a passion for learning. Shannon lives close to Niagara Falls and enjoys vacationing in the Muskokas with her family.